# QUILTS
## from the
# SELVAGE EDGE

Karen Griska

**American Quilter's Society**

P. O. Box 3290 • Paducah, KY 42002-3290

*www.americanquilter.com*

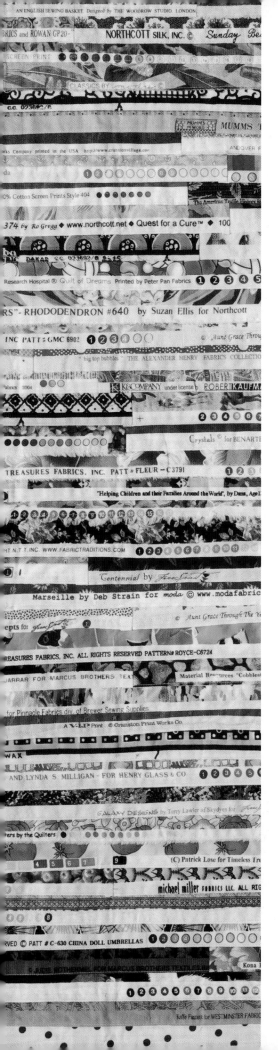

The American Quilter's Society (AQS), located in Paducah, Kentucky, is dedicated to promoting the accomplishments of today's quilters. Through its publications and events, AQS strives to honor today's quiltmakers and their work and to inspire future creativity and innovation in quiltmaking.

Text © 2008, Author, Karen Griska
Artwork © 2008 American Quilter's Society

Executive Editor: Nicole C. Chambers
Editor: Linda Baxter Lasco
Graphic Design: Lynda Smith
Cover Design: Michael Buckingham
Photography: Charles R. Lynch
Photo of Mark Lipinski & Tulip by Jeff MacWright
Karen Griska's photo by James Kriegsmann, Jr.

**American Quilter's Society**
P. O. Box 3290 • Paducah, KY 42002-3290
*www.americanquilter.com*

Additional copies of this book may be ordered from the American Quilter's Society, PO Box 3290, Paducah, KY 42002-3290, or online at: www.AmericanQuilter.com.

Library of Congress Cataloging-in-Publication Data

Griska, Karen.
 Quilts from the selvage edge / by Karen Griska.
   p. cm.
 ISBN 978-1-57432-957-5
 1. Strip quilting--Patterns. 2. Patchwork--Patterns. I. Title.

TT835.G765 2008
746.46'041--dc22

                                        2008010328

*Proudly printed and bound in the United States of America.*

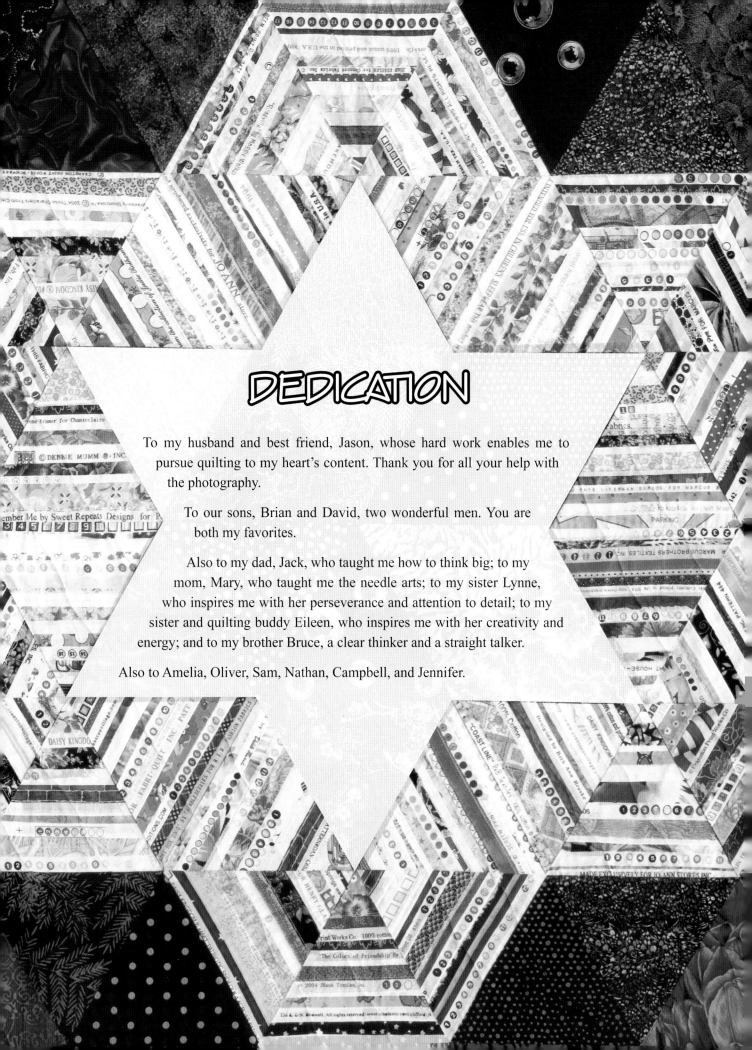

# DEDICATION

To my husband and best friend, Jason, whose hard work enables me to pursue quilting to my heart's content. Thank you for all your help with the photography.

To our sons, Brian and David, two wonderful men. You are both my favorites.

Also to my dad, Jack, who taught me how to think big; to my mom, Mary, who taught me the needle arts; to my sister Lynne, who inspires me with her perseverance and attention to detail; to my sister and quilting buddy Eileen, who inspires me with her creativity and energy; and to my brother Bruce, a clear thinker and a straight talker.

Also to Amelia, Oliver, Sam, Nathan, Campbell, and Jennifer.

# ACKNOWLEDGMENTS

I would like to thank the following quilters for contributing
their selvages and encouragement to this project:

Anita & Jim Augeri, Lansdale, Pennsylvania

Nancy Bishoff, Dresher, Pennsylvania

Carol Breinig, North Wales, Pennsylvania

Sarah Donnelly, Rumford, Rhode Island

Sue Edelman, Abington, Pennsylvania

Linda Eichhorn, Doylestown, Pennsylvania

Gertrude Gojeski, Carversville, Pennsylvania

Barbara Harrison, Doylestown, Pennsylvania

Cita Jacobs, Doylestown, Pennsylvania

Cassandra Jeter, Doylestown, Pennsylvania

Ellen Johnson, Chalfont, Pennsylvania

Barbara Lewis, Elkins Park, Pennsylvania

Eileen Lovett, East Providence, Rhode Island

Jeanne Malone, Lansdale, Pennsylvania

Gwen Marston, Beaver Island, Michigan

Terri Mellor, Fort Washington, Pennsylvania

Mary Montanye, Chalfont, Pennsylvania

The Newman Piecemakers
of Rumford, Rhode Island

Ann Pignatelli, Buckingham, Pennsylvania

Jane Prole, Bay of Plenty, New Zealand

Dana Richterova, Czech Republic

Suzanne Sergeant, Doylestown, Pennsylvania

Pam & Elizabeth Stahl, Franklin, Tennessee

Kyoko Takeuchi, Maple Glen, Pennsylvania

Clarice Teare, Noblesville, Indiana

Helen Wolf, Doylestown, Pennsylvania

# TABLE OF CONTENTS

# FOREWORD

*It wasn't pretty.*

*When I was first turned on to Karen Griska's amazing selvage quilts, I immediately crumpled into a sobbing mass on my studio floor. All of those fabric selvages I cut and carelessly tossed into the trash throughout all the years I've been quiltmaking! I was breathless at the very thought of all those unborn quilt tops I'd callously dumped! Oh, the inhumanity! (Oh, the waste!)*

*Yet, once I pulled my quivering self back together and dried my tears, I was truly astonished by the creativity and the powerful statements in Karen's handiwork. Most of us see zilch in a strip of selvage, but Karen sees bits of color and letter forms and a way to arrange them into simple and attention-grabbing quilt designs. These bits and scraps speak to her. She's a master of the discarded, the champion of trash. This Ultimate Scrap Queen recognized something that nobody else saw: beauty in the details.*

*Kids, with this book, Karen has established herself as a quiltmaking visionary, teaching us to see unique and simple beauty in the selvages that we have always just thrown away. It's a huge lesson in learning to be receptive to everything around us and coaching us to see shining potential in the unremarkable. Through her work and designs, we are inspired to see the relationship between even our most insignificant fabric crumbs and our quiltmaking through enlightened eyes.*

*And there's another bonus: In our modern age of "green living," we piecemakers can be proud of the fact that we were the original recyclers. For literally centuries, people, we've used worn clothing, rags, and scraps to make quilt tops, and old blankets and coats—even newspapers—for batting. Say*

*what you want, but we have done our share to save the planet. (Are ya hearing me, Al?) Now we can save the beauty of the discarded as well.*

*With Karen's inspiration, we can use every itty bitty piece of our fabric by incorporating even the selvages into traditional and not-so-traditional quilts with stunning and ecologically important results. (And as every scrap diva worth the name knows, every little bit truly helps.) When we channel our inner recycler by making selvage quilts, we're staying connected with quilting history. It's our contemporary way of keeping quiltmaking as pure as those quilters who collected discarded pieces of fabric long before the rotary cutter was a gleam in Olfa's eye. (Did I mention the fact that you are actually saving some stash cash, too?)*

*My dears, forget about what you know and how to do it. This book and these designs are about possibility and forward thinking. They'll take you from the humdrum of typical quilting pattern books into a new way of looking at your craft and the world. It's about seeing usefulness in the useless and multifaceted design in easy simplicity.*

*So, as soon as you've picked yourself up off the floor after being stricken with grief over the years of selvages lost, let yourself embrace the excitement, the spark, the renewal that Karen gives you in these pages.*

*And hey—gotta go! I've got selvages to sew!*

**Mark Lipinski**
Mark Lipinski's Quilter's Home *magazine*
*www.quiltershomemag.com*

# INTRODUCTION

Anyone who has been a quilter longer than a week probably has a fabric stash. You may not have thought about this, but you have a wealth of selvages!

We quilters have fabrics that we are saving for special projects, fabrics that go with our UFOs (unfinished objects), yardage we bought on sale, and treasures we found at quilt shows. We have souvenirs from our various quilting phases—novelty fabrics, landscape prints, 1930s' prints, brights, florals, antique reproduction fabrics, and so on. We have fabrics that make us wonder what we were thinking that day. You probably have miles of selvages.

### Why would anyone want to make a selvage quilt?

Because it's fun and you can enjoy your whole stash and not use any of it up! If you don't like your creation, who cares? You were just going to throw the selvages away, anyway.

It's creative. You can make almost any kind of quilt using selvages. The "Quilt Police" haven't established any rules of decency in this category so feel free to put your William Morris fabric near your Strawberry Shortcake fabric if you want to.

They're beautiful. Like other scrap quilts, selvage quilts have a busy appearance. The eye dances all over the quilt, taking in all the details. Selvages make dazzling wall quilts and throws.

They are fun to read. Do your selvages have copyright dates or the names of the designers? Do the patterns have interesting names? Do you have any selvages written in a foreign language?

They're sturdy. Selvage quilts are not just interesting conversation pieces. They make great utility quilts.

It may be that the best part is hearing your quilting friends say "selvage quilts?" If your friends don't appreciate selvage quilts, that's wonderful! Ask them to give you their selvages.

When you finish your selvage quilt, e-mail a photo of you and your quilt to www.SelvageQuilts.com and it will be added to an online exhibit. Visit often to see what other quilters have made.

### What are selvages all about?

If you are new to the world of fabrics, you may not know what selvages are nor what information is found on them. The two long woven edges running the length of a fabric are the selvages. The threads are folded over so that the fabric will not unravel during the manufacturing and printing process. As a result, the selvage is denser than the rest of the fabric. This is why quilters normally start by trimming and discarding the selvages.

Many selvages have printing on them, but not all. Solid colored fabrics generally have none. The same is true for antique fabrics and some fabrics made outside of the United States. Generally selvages can include the name of the manufacturer and, in recent years, their Web site address. You'll often see the name of the artist who created the design, and the name of the fabric collection or the individual design. A copyright symbol and the year of introduction are common. Sometimes the fiber content is included.

The color dots, or color windows, show all the colors used in printing the fabric. Each rotary screen used in the printing process applies one color to the fabric and corresponds to one color dot. There may be as many as sixteen screens used to print a fabric. The registration marks, little + or # marks on the selvage, aid the proper positioning of the rotary screens so the colors will print in the right spot.

# GETTING STARTED:
## CHOOSING AND CUTTING SELVAGES

**1  How should I cut the selvages?**

Cut your selvages about 1½" wide so some of the printed fabric will show when you sew your selvages to foundation fabric. That width is easier to handle than a narrower strip. Cut with scissors or a rotary cutter, whichever you prefer. Speed is more important than neatness at this stage. However, don't tear off the selvages. Tearing distorts the strips, making them hard to use.

**2  What quantity of selvages will I need to make a quilt?**

How much you need depends on how you answer some of the following questions. You may want to start by trimming some of the more interesting or colorful selvages from your stash, then start arranging the selvages onto foundation fabric. You will soon get an idea of the quantity you need. In general, when you have a one-gallon plastic storage bag full of selvages, you'll have enough to make any of the quilts in this book.

**3  Should I use both selvages or only the one that has writing and color dots?**

It's your quilt, so you are the boss. If you have an abundance of selvages, you may decide not to use the plain ones. I like to add some plain selvages to the mix. I also use some selvages that have no white stripe at all. The pattern continues right up to the edge of the fabric. That made it easy to create the dark selvage areas in the GLASS TUMBLING BLOCKS quilt (see page 44).

**4  If the edge of a selvage is shaggy, should I use it?**

I think the shaggy edges of some selvages add interest and I like to use them. Although they are shaggy, it is a bound, not a raw, edge and it will not unravel. When you press your blocks, these "shaggies" can get pushed one way, then the other. I like how that looks, so this doesn't bother me. Take a look at the close-up photos and decide for yourself.

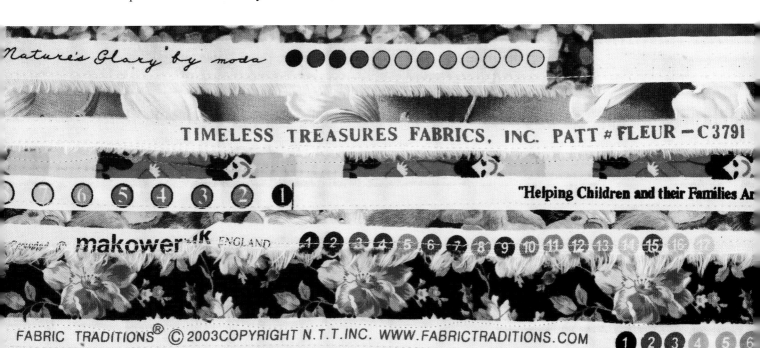

**What if my selvage isn't long enough to cover the distance I need?**
Simply join two or three selvage lengths, right sides together, if the strip you're using isn't long enough. I used this method in the quilt SURPRISE (page 26).

**What if I need lots of selvages?**
Alert your quilting buddies and your guild members. If your local quilt shop makes kits, they may save selvages for you. Search the Internet for quilters who want to swap fabrics. I have received selvages from New Zealand and the Czech Republic this way. Be clear that you want the selvages to be about 1½" (or 4 cm.) wide. Now that the word is out, I have selvages arriving all the time.

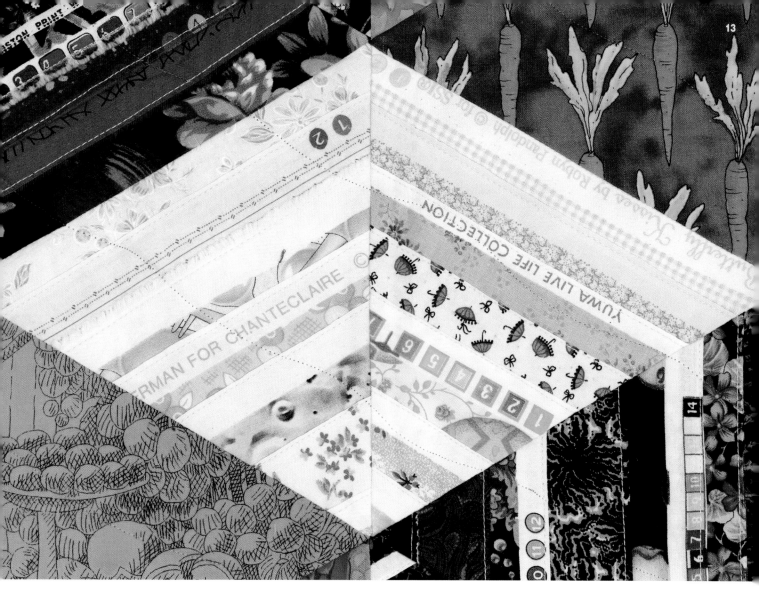

 **What if I decide that I need to rip out a selvage?**

Selvages are very stretch-resistant, so it is surprisingly easy to rip one out of a block. Using a seam ripper, carefully remove the stitches in both seams holding the selvage to the foundation fabric. Gently tug it out. Insert another strip and stitch it in place.

**8** **What if the writing on some of my selvages is upside-down in a certain design?**

In some instances, that is how it has to be. For example, the light selvages in GLASS TUMBLING BLOCKS (page 44) are all upside-down, as are some of the selvages in ACRES OF AFTERNOON (page 46). If you like all your words right-side-up, keep an eye on that as you work at your design wall.

*Are selvage quilts washable?*

The blocks shown in the instruction photos in The Basics were used to make a small quilt to find the answer to this question. The quilt was photographed in new condition. It was very flat, and had a nice crisp feel, like most new and unwashed quilts.

First, I washed the quilt by hand in cool water with a little dishwashing liquid. Then, it was laid flat to dry. It puckered just a little bit, as most washed quilts do.

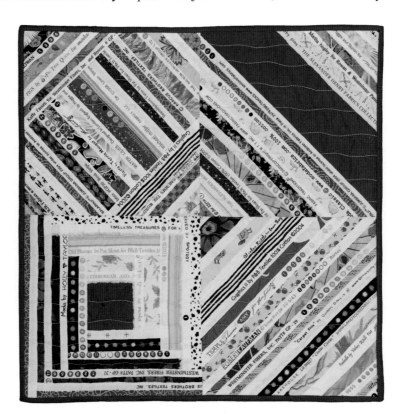

Second, I washed it by machine with a regular load of laundry. I used warm water and laundry detergent with color-safe bleach. Then I dried it in the dryer on a medium heat setting, although in my opinion that gets pretty hot. In this process, the quilt received no special attention, like most utility quilts. This time, the quilt came out significantly more puckered and softer, but definitely not distorted or undesirable in any way.

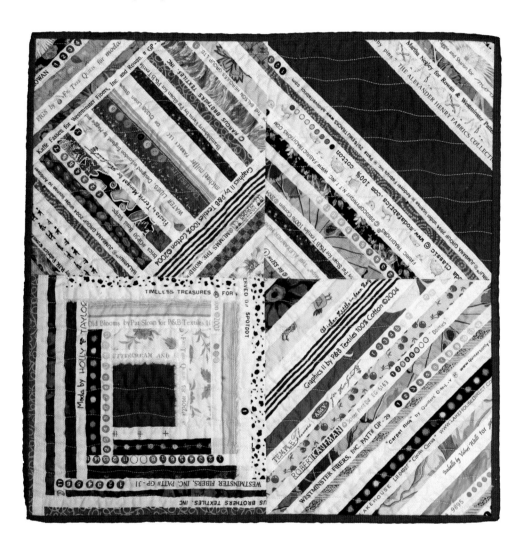

Happily, I concluded that a selvage quilt can definitely be washed, and even be used as a utility quilt.

# THE BASICS:
## HOW TO MAKE SELVAGE BLOCKS

### *General Instructions*

Choose a good quality muslin for the foundation fabric. You can substitute one of your "uglies" for the muslin yardage called for in the projects because the foundation will be completely covered by the selvages.

The bound edge of the first selvage should align with the edge of the foundation fabric. A generous overlap of the bound edge of the second and subsequent selvage strips will ensure that you secure the raw edge of the preceding selvage.

You may want to hold selvage strips in place with pins at first, but with a little practice, you won't need pins.

### *Making a Square*

Cut a foundation square the size of your choice.

Cut selvage strips a little longer than the width of your foundation fabric.

Lay a selvage strip along the bottom edge of the square, lining up the bound edge of the selvage with the edge of the square. Sew along the bound edge of the selvage as shown.

Lay selvage #2 on top of selvage #1, covering the raw edge of selvage #1. (This is the only rule in selvage quilting!) Sew selvage #2 along the bound edge.

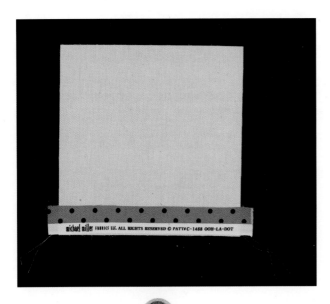

Continue adding selvage strips until the foundation square is covered. The last selvage can hang off the top edge.

Trim off any excess using a rotary cutter and ruler or template.

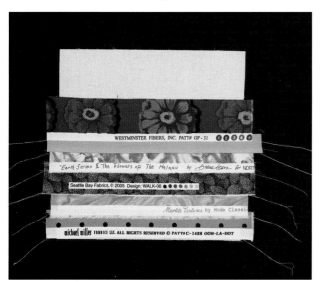

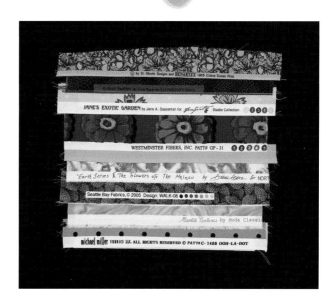

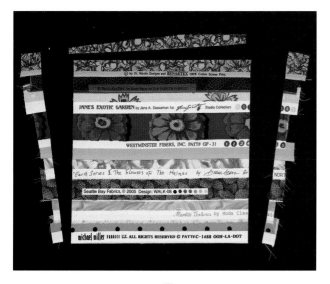

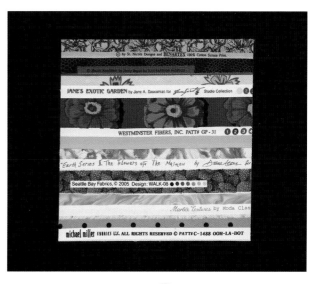

### *Making a Square – Diagonal Variation*

Cut a foundation square the size of your choice. Draw a diagonal line on the foundation square to help you align the selvages diagonally or simply place the selvages "by eye."

Use a short selvage for the first strip, starting in a corner. Sew a short seam along the bottom edge of this selvage. Adding the next selvage will help secure the first piece. When sewing selvage #2 to the block, be sure to sew through the raw top edge of selvage #1.

Continue, as shown in the illustrations, until the foundation square is covered. Trim the overhanging selvage ends.

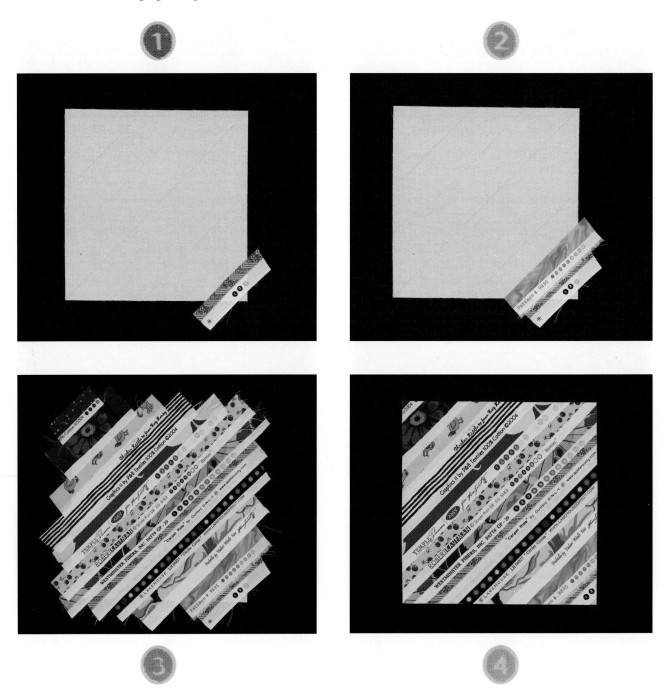

### Making Half-Square Triangles

Cut a square from the fabric that you want to show on the "not selvage-covered" half. In this illustration, as in the TREE OF LIFE quilt (page 34), that is the red fabric.

Lay a selvage strip diagonally across the square, as shown. Sew the bound edge. Lay selvage #2 on top of selvage #1, covering the raw edge of #1. Sew.

Continue in this manner, as shown in the illustration. Trim.

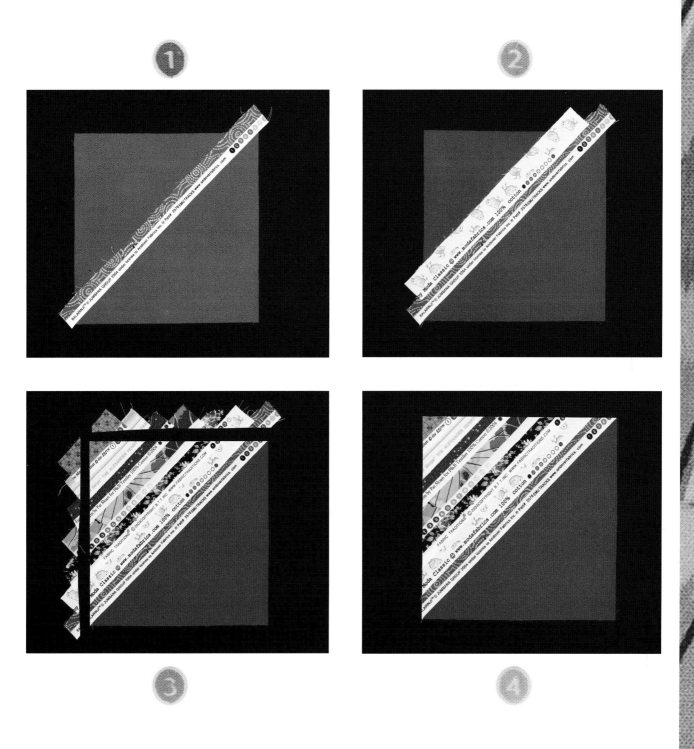

### Making Half-Square Triangles – Variation

Starting with a half-square triangle, cover a little bit of the opposite corner as shown below. Trim.

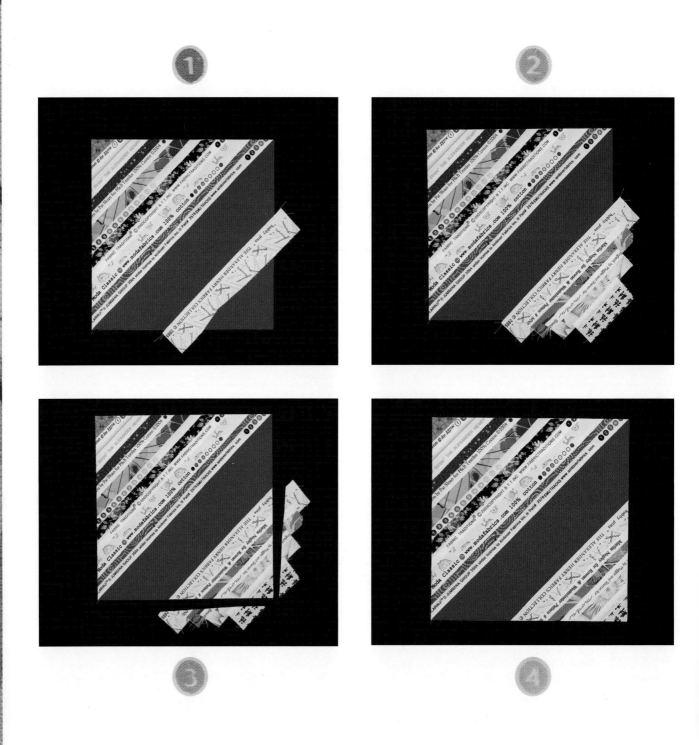

## *Making Long Blocks*

Cut a foundation strip the width of your choice. In this example, the strip is 6 inches wide.

Cover the foundation strip one selvage at a time, as shown below. Continue to the desired length.

You can piece the foundation fabric to make it longer since the seam will not show in the finished block. Trim as shown below.

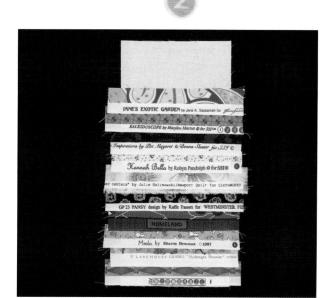

### *Making Equilateral Triangles*

To cut foundation fabric for your equilateral triangles, first cut a strip the width of the desired height of the triangle.

Square off one end using your rotary ruler and cutter.

Align the 30-degree line on your rotary ruler with the squared end of the strip and cut along the edge of the ruler .

Align the 60-degree line on your rotary ruler with the cut end of the strip and cut along the edge of the ruler for your first equilateral triangle.

Continue cutting triangles by aligning the 60-degree line with end of the strip.

One side of the triangle is cut on the straight of the grain. The other two sides have bias (stretchy) edges.

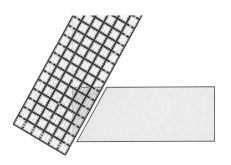 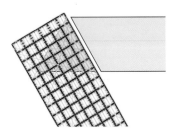 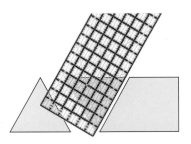

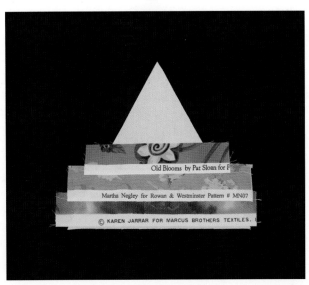 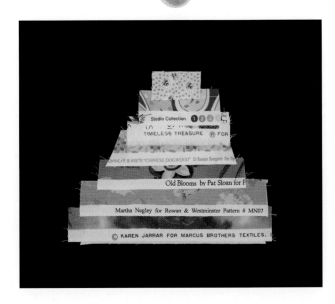

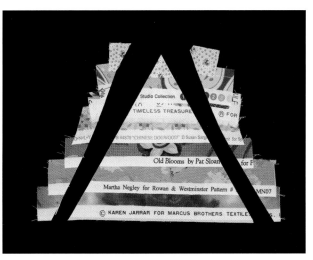 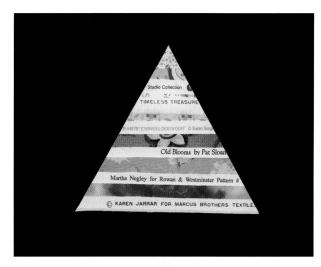

Apply the selvages parallel to the non-stretchy, straight-of-grain edge, as shown. If you forget this step, the resulting curly triangle will be a handy reminder! Continue adding selvage strips until the foundation fabric is completely covered. Trim.

### Using a Design Wall

You will be amazed by the designs that emerge when you start playing with quilt blocks on your design wall. To make a design wall, buy 5 yards of solid off-white flannel. Cut it into two 2½ yard pieces. Sew them together lengthwise as if you were making quilt backing. Thumbtack the flannel to a wall. Quilt blocks adhere nicely without pinning. You will love this giant workspace. The ability to view your designs-in-progress from a distance will energize you to new creative heights! This is how I discovered the design for TWILIGHT STAR (page 42).

### Working with Selvage Blocks

Stay open to new design possibilities as you work. This is how I get my best ideas. Ask yourself:

● What if I turn some of these blocks upside-down?

● What if I reverse the dark and light areas?

● What if I cover hexagons with selvages?

● How would it look if I used variegated thread to sew the selvages onto the foundation fabric?

If your quilt calls for sewing two selvage-covered foundation pieces together, it may get bulky. This can cause the fabric on top to pass under the presser foot of the sewing machine a little slower than the fabric on the bottom. I have found that using the quilter's walking foot helps prevent this slippage.

In ACRES OF AFTERNOON, there are some places where two selvage-covered blocks meet in a slightly awkward way. The selvages are on an angle and there is plenty of bulk. This is a perfect time to use a walking foot.

*Hint: Lay a bath towel on your ironing surface before pressing your seams to one side. This way, any bulky seam intersections will nestle into the towel, and the finished quilt top will lie nice and flat.*

To avoid dealing with bulky intersections at all, just add a narrow border to separate two selvage-covered areas of your design, as shown below. I like the look of black-and-white fabrics combined with selvages.

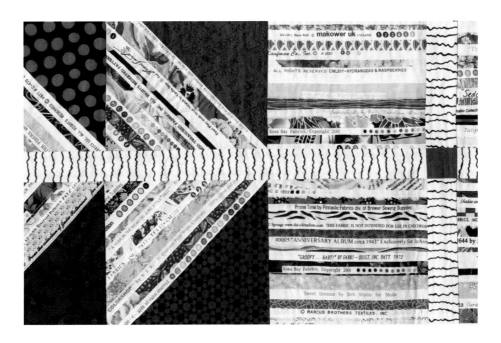

Include some eye-catching fabrics: something bright, some big polka dots, or a surprise. This quilt has some cows near the selvage. If you cut your selvages wide enough, you can take advantage of these little surprises.

Karen Griska

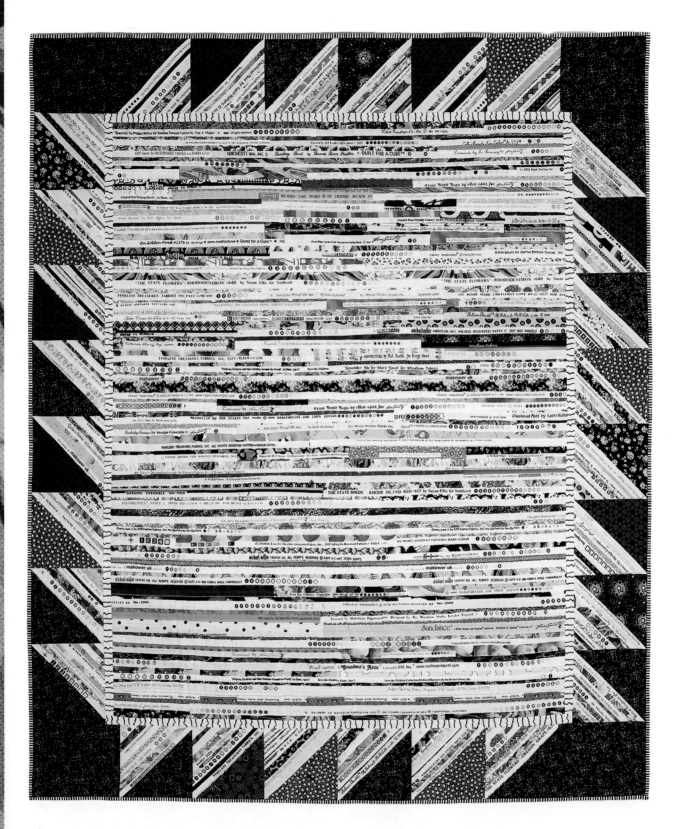

# Surprise • 47" x 57" • *Made and quilted by the author*

This is the quilt that started it all. It was made in response to a call for entries for an exhibit of "recycled art." At first, I just planned to cover a rectangle of muslin and add binding. The "Aha!" moment came when I realized that I could make half-square triangles for a nice border. That was the surprise! If you can make half-square triangles, you can make countless quilt designs. From that moment on, one idea led to another.

## Foundation Fabric for Center Rectangle

1⅜ yards

36" x 45" rectangle

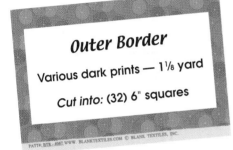

## Narrow Inner Border

Black & White — ¼ yard

Cut into: (5) 1½" x 40" strips;

piece to fit

## Outer Border

Various dark prints — 1⅛ yard

Cut into: (32) 6" squares

## Straight-grain Double-fold Binding

B & W — ½ yard

Cut into: (6) 2½" x 40" strips

## Quilt Backing

4 yards

Cut into: (2) 2 yard lengths

## Batting

55" x 65"

### Sewing Instructions

Cover the muslin rectangle with selvages as shown in Making a Square (page 16). Piece selvage strips end-to-end to make longer strips, as needed. Trim the edges.

Add a small inner border with the black-and-white 1½" strips.

This small border lets you avoid having to sew two selvage-covered blocks together. It also gives the eye a place to rest. I think black-and-white fabrics look particularly nice with selvages.

Set aside 4 of the dark print 6" squares for cornerstones.

Cover half of each of the remaining 6" squares with selvages diagonally, using the method shown in Making Half-Square Triangles (page 19).

Sew 8 blocks together for the side borders and add to the quilt.

"Tweak" the borders as necessary by increasing the seam allowances between blocks to shorten them or by adding scraps of dark fabric on the ends to lengthen them. This imprecise approach adds to the charming, casual look of selvage quilts.

Sew 6 blocks together for the top and bottom borders, adding one of the remaining plain squares to each end. Add to the quilt.

Layer the quilt top, batting, and backing. Quilt as desired. Square up the quilt top and bind.

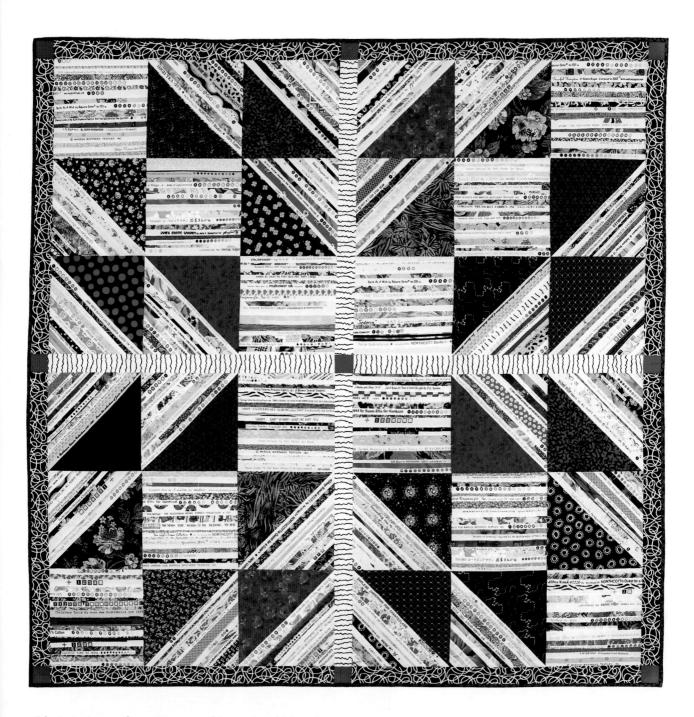

# Old Maid's Puzzle, Solved  •  56" x 56"  •  *Made and quilted by the author*

This arrangement of the Old Maid's Puzzle block was so satisfying and had such a classic look that I had to declare this puzzle finally solved. You may also see it as a Variable Star variation.

## Foundation Fabric Complete Blocks

⅞ yard

Cut into: (12) 9" squares

## Half-covered Blocks

Dark fabrics — 1¾ yards

Cut into: (24) 9" squares

## Sashing

Black-and-White — ⅜ yard

Cut into: (4) 2" x 27" strips

## Red Squares

Red — ⅛ yard

Cut into: (9) 2" squares

## Border

Black-and-White — ¾ yard

Cut into: (8) 2" x 27" strips

## Straight-grain Double-fold Binding

Black/dark grey print — ½ yard

Cut into: (6) 2½" x 40" strips

## Quilt Back

3¾ yards

Cut into: (2) 1⅞ yard lengths

## Batting

64" x 64"

### Sewing Instructions

Cover the 12 foundation fabric 9" squares with selvages as shown in Making a Square (page 16).

Cover half of each of the dark 9" squares diagonally with selvages, as shown in Making Half-Square Triangles (page 19). Assemble the squares into 4 Old Maid's Puzzle blocks, as shown.

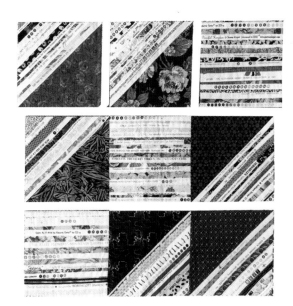

Sew the blocks, sashing strips, outer border strips, and red square cornerstones into rows as shown. Join the rows.

Layer the quilt top with the backing and batting and quilt. Square up the quilt top and use the 2½" strips to bind the raw edges of your quilt.

# Cow Barns, Night Skies • 62" x 62" • *Made and quilted by the author*

Always attracted to Schoolhouse block quilts, I thought the half-square triangles would make nice roofs for buildings. My cow fabrics inspired me to see these buildings as barns. The dazzling fabrics used for the skies needed honorable mention in the title, too.

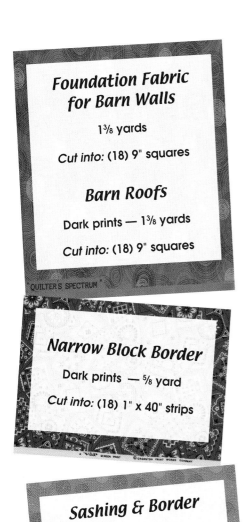

## Foundation Fabric for Barn Walls

1⅜ yards

*Cut into:* (18) 9" squares

## Barn Roofs

Dark prints — 1⅜ yards

*Cut into:* (18) 9" squares

## Narrow Block Border

Dark prints — ⅝ yard

*Cut into:* (18) 1" x 40" strips

## Sashing & Border

B&W prints — 1 yard

*Cut into:* (13) 2½" x 40" strips

## Straight-grain Double-fold Binding

½ yard

*Cut into:* (7) 2½" x 40" strips

## Quilt Back

4 yards

*Cut into:* (2) 2 yard lengths

## Batting

70" x 70"

### Sewing Instructions

Cover the 18 fabric squares with selvages as shown in Making a Square (page 16). Cover half of each of the dark 9" squares diagonally with selvages, see Making Half-Square Triangles (page 19).

Assemble the blocks into barns. Add a 1" border to each Barn block.

Cut 6 sashing pieces from the 2½" wide strips the length of the blocks. Join with the blocks into rows.

My two-fabric sashing is the result of not having enough of either of the cow fabrics, but I like the result.

Piece the remaining sashing strips end-to-end. Measure the rows through the center and cut 4 strips to that measurement. Join the long sashing strips with the rows.

Measure the length of the quilt. Cut 2 sashing strips to that measurement and add to the sides of the quilt.

Layer the quilt top with the backing and batting and quilt. Square up the quilt top and bind.

# Gems on Point • 56" x 56" • *Made and quilted by the author*

This quilt design emerged on the design wall as I played with the barn roofs. Very often one quilt leads to the next. I like the way the four little gems are set in the center of the quilt.

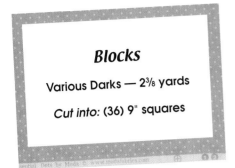

## Blocks

Various Darks — 2⅜ yards

*Cut into:* (36) 9" squares

## Border

Dark Print — ½ yard

*Cut into:* (5) 3" x 40" strips

## Straight-grain Double-fold Binding

Dark Print — ½ yard

*Cut into:* (6) 2½" x 40" strips

## Quilt Backing

3¾ yards

*Cut into:* (2) 1⅞ yard lengths

## Batting

64" x 64"

### Sewing Instructions

Cover half of each of the 9" dark print squares diagonally with selvages, as shown in Making Half-Square Triangles (page 19).

On 16 of these squares, add selvages to part of the opposite corner to make the small gems as shown in Making Half-Square Triangles – Variation (page 20).

Arrange the blocks with the 20 half-plain blocks around the outside edges. Sew the blocks into rows, then join the rows.

You may want to use your quilter's walking foot to piece these squares because of the bulk where two selvage-covered blocks meet. Use a towel on your ironing surface to accommodate the bulk so that your attached blocks will lie nice and flat.

Add a border using the 3" wide strips.

Layer the quilt top with the backing and batting and quilt. Square up the quilt top and use the 2½" strips to bind the raw edges of your quilt.

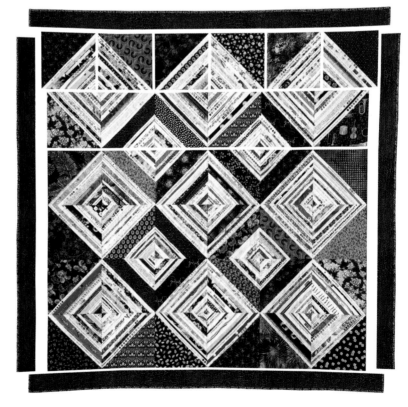

QUILTS FROM THE SELVAGE EDGE

Karen Griska

# Tree of Life • 48" x 48" • *Made and quilted by the author*

This quilt is one of my all-time favorites. Done in red, it is reminiscent of the old red and white quilts, adding to its classic beauty. Who would have guessed that the elegant Tree of Life block would look so good done in selvages?

The red binding makes a delicate frame for this quilt. Save some nice long selvages for the large corner triangles.

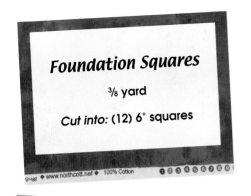

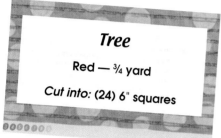

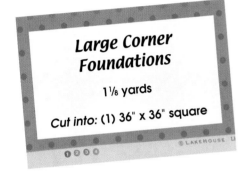

### Sewing Instructions

Completely cover the 6" squares of muslin with selvages diagonally, as shown in Making a Square – Diagonal Variation (page 18).

Cover half of each of the 22 of the red 6" squares diagonally with selvages, as shown in Making Half-Square Triangles (page 19).

Arrange the blocks and the 2 remaining plain red squares as shown.

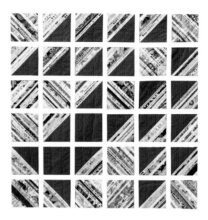

Cut a square of muslin two inches bigger than your tree, about 36" x 36". Draw an X on this square, from corner to corner, and cut on these 2 lines, as in the illustration.

Cover these large triangles with selvages using the same method as shown in Making Equilateral Triangles (page 22).

Turn the tree on point and attach the 4 corner triangles. Trim so that the quilt is square.

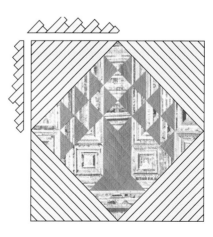

Layer the quilt top with the backing and batting and quilt. Square up the quilt top and use the 2½" strips to bind the raw edges of your quilt.

Karen Griska

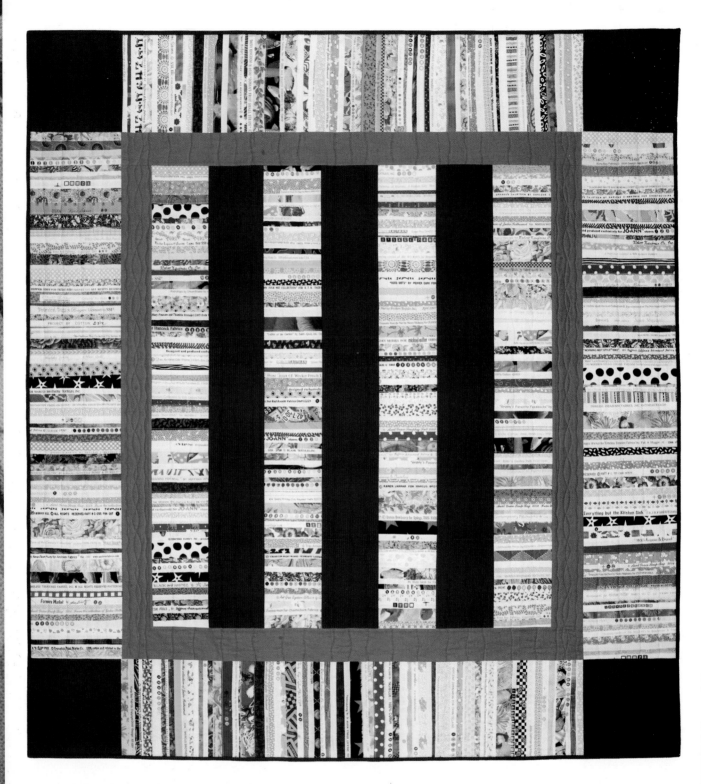

# Amish at Heart • 53" x 56" • *Made and quilted by the author*

This quilt was a challenge to see how versatile selvage quilting could be. By paying attention to the classic elements of Amish quilt design, it comes close to an Amish-style quilt, if only "at heart." You will be delighted to see how quickly you can make these long blocks.

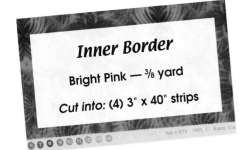

## Selvage Foundations

1¾ yards

Cut into: (4) 5" x 35" strips

(4) 8½" x 41" strips

## Dark Strips, Cornerstones & Straight-grain Double-fold Binding

Dark Solid — 1⅛ yards

Cut into: (3) 5" x 35" strips

Cornerstones (4) 8½" squares

Binding (6) 2½" x 40" strips

## Inner Border

Bright Pink — ⅜ yard

Cut into: (4) 3" x 40" strips

## Quilt Back

3¾ yards

Cut into: (2) 1⅞ yard lengths

## Batting

61" x 64"

### Sewing Instructions

Cover the 5" wide foundation strips with selvages as shown in Making Long Blocks (page 21). Then, join the selvage-pieced strips with the 5" wide solid dark strips to make the center of the quilt.

Add the 3" wide inner border strips as illustrated.

Cover the four 8½" wide foundation strips with selvages for your borders.

Measure the length and width of the quilt through the center and trim the covered strips to that measurement. Add to the sides of the quilt.

Sew a dark 8½" square to both ends of the remaining borders and add to the top and bottom of the quilt.

Layer the quilt top with the backing and batting and quilt as desired. Square up the quilt top and bind.

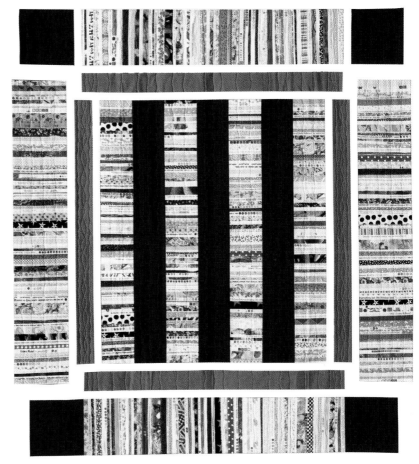

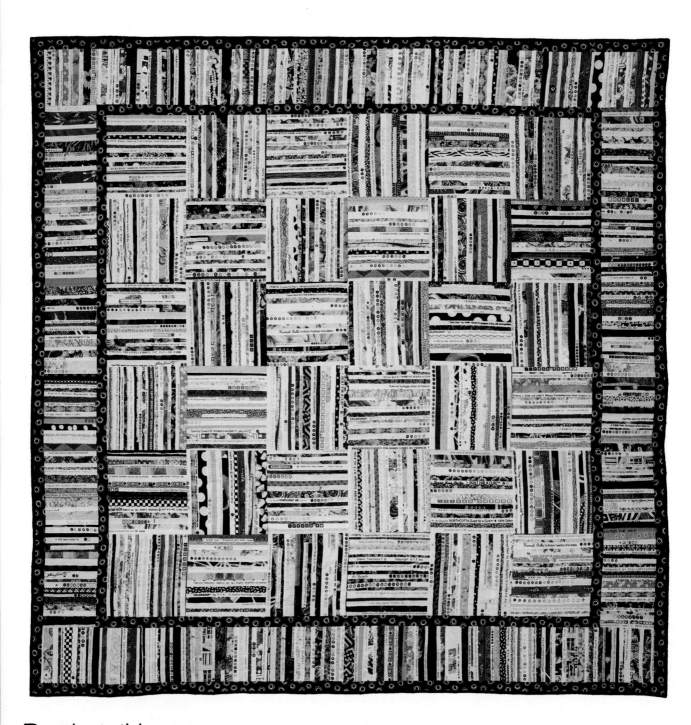

# Basket Weave • 66" x 66" • *Made and quilted by the author*

Sometimes I call this quilt BASKET WEAVE FOR OVERACHIEVERS because it is so big and dazzling. I made it big because I was having so much fun making these blocks. It was not a matter of grit and determination, although my non-quilting friends don't believe me when I say this. I love the woven look of this quilt.

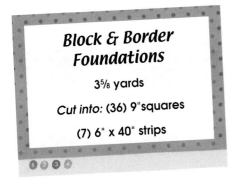

**Block & Border
Foundations**

3⅝ yards

Cut into: (36) 9"squares

(7) 6" x 40" strips

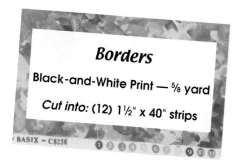

**Borders**

Black-and-White Print — ⅝ yard

Cut into: (12) 1½" x 40" strips

**Straight-grain
Double-fold Binding**

Black — ⅝ yard

Cut into: (7) 2½" x 40" strips

**Quilt Back**

4½ yards

Cut into: (2) 2¼ yard lengths

**Batting**

74" x 74"

## Sewing Instructions

Cover the 36 foundation squares with selvages as shown in Making a Square (page 16).

Arrange the squares in 6 rows of 6 blocks each, alternating the orientation of the blocks as illustrated. Sew the blocks into rows, then join the rows.

Add an inner border using the 1½" wide strips.

Piece the remaining 6" wide foundation strips. Cut two pieces 56" and two pieces 66" long. Cover with selvages as shown in Making Long Blocks (page 21).

Measure the length of the quilt through the center, and cut the 56" covered strips to that measurement. Add to the sides of the quilt.

Measure the width of the quilt through the center, and cut the 66" covered strips to that measurement. Add to the top and bottom of the quilt. Add the final border using the remaining 1½" wide strips.

Layer the quilt top, batting, and backing. Quilt as desired. Square up the quilt top and bind.

QUILTS FROM THE SELVAGE EDGE

Karen Griska

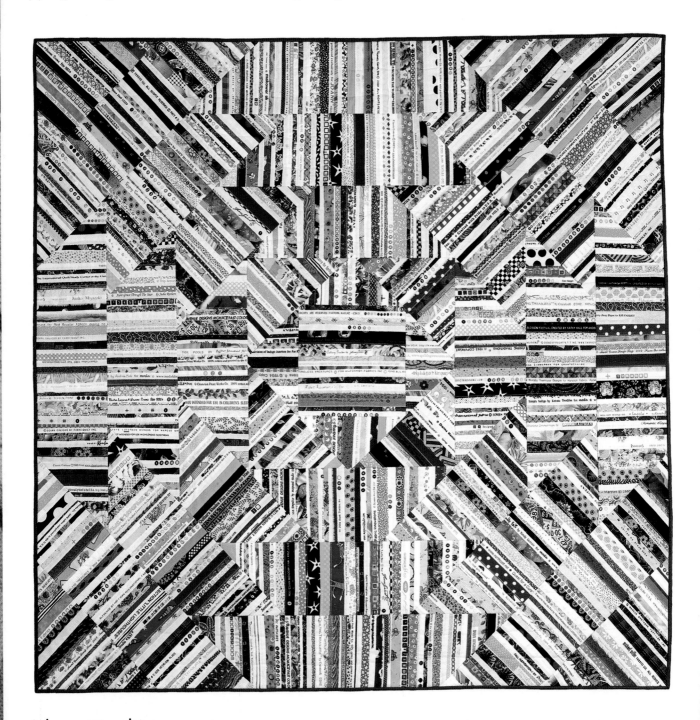

# Hospitality • 50" x 50" • *Made and quilted by the author*

This quilt is one big Pineapple block, the symbol of hospitality. Long ago, when ship captains returned home to the island of Nantucket, off the coast of Massachusetts, they would put a pineapple on their front gate post, indicating to the neighbors that they were home from the sea. I suspect there are other versions of the story behind the pineapple symbol, but this is the story I was told in Nantucket.

Like AMISH AT HEART, this quilt is made from long strips covered with selvages.

I love this quilt because it looks so difficult to make, but it isn't! I learned how to make a Pineapple block from Loretta Smith's book, *Pineapple Quilt, A Piece of Cake*. I highly recommend this book. She shows how to make a precision block, but once you get the idea, you can make them "by eye."

## Sewing Instructions

Cover the center foundation square with selvages as shown in Making a Square (page 16).

Cut 4 segments from the 6" wide strips of foundation fabric about ½" longer than the center square. Cover the strips with selvages as shown in Making Long Blocks (page 21).

Sew them to the four sides of the center square as shown.

Position the edge of the ruler so that a little of each corner of the center block is cut off.

Trim the sides by aligning the 45-degree angle line on your ruler with the side of the center square.

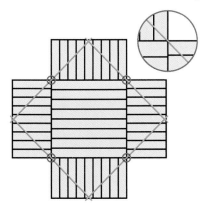

Measure the sides of the new square and cut 4 segments from the 6" wide strips of foundation fabric about ½" longer than that measurement.

Cover these strips with selvages and sew them to the four sides of the square.

Trim as before, again cutting off a little of the corners of the previous square, indicated in red.

Don't worry that the four areas marked in green are "empty." This is part of the design and works out as you add subsequent rounds.

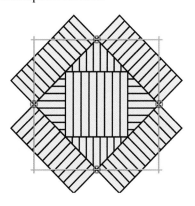

*Hint: Use the biggest square template you have to help square-up your quilt top as you add each successive round.*

Repeat these steps another 6 times. The final round (the ninth) is added to the same 4 sides as the preceding round. Otherwise, this would be "The Quilt That Never Ends!"

Layer the quilt top, batting, and backing and quilt as desired. Square up the quilt top and bind.

# Twlight Star  •  49" x 51"  •  *Made and quilted by the author*

I discovered this star as I played at my design wall. That kind of experience is what keeps me excited about quilting! To add sparkle, I used many of my selvages that contain color dots.

I made one blue and one red border, just for fun. I think the black-and-white striped binding nicely complements the black and white in the selvage star.

## Foundation Fabric for Selvage-covered Triangles

1⅛ yards

*Cut into:* (5) 6¾" x 40" strips, then cut 36 equilateral triangles

## Star Center & Dark Background

Dark prints — 2¼ yards

*Cut into:* (11) 6¾" x 40" strips, then cut 84 equilateral triangles

## Top Border

Dark print — ⅛ yard

*Cut into:* (2) 1¾" x 42" strips

## Bottom Border

Dark print — ⅛ yard

*Cut into:* (2) 1¾" x 42" strips

## Straight-grain Double-fold Binding

B & W stripe — ½ yard

*Cut into:* (6) 2½" x 42" strips

## Quilt Backing

3½ yards

*Cut into:* (2) 1¾ yard lengths

## Batting

57" x 59"

### Sewing Instructions

Cover the 36 foundation fabric triangles with selvages, starting at the straight-of-grain edge, as shown in Making Equilateral Triangles (page 22).

Arrange the selvage-covered and plain triangles on your design wall as shown.

Keep an eye on the direction of the selvages if you like the "pie slice" effect, as in this quilt.

Sew the triangles together in rows, then join the rows. Trim off the zigzag edge on the right and left sides of the quilt.

Add a 1¾" border to the top and the bottom to avoid having the top and bottom star points touch the binding.

Layer the quilt top with the backing and batting and quilt. Square up the quilt top and use the 2½" strips to bind the raw edges of your quilt.

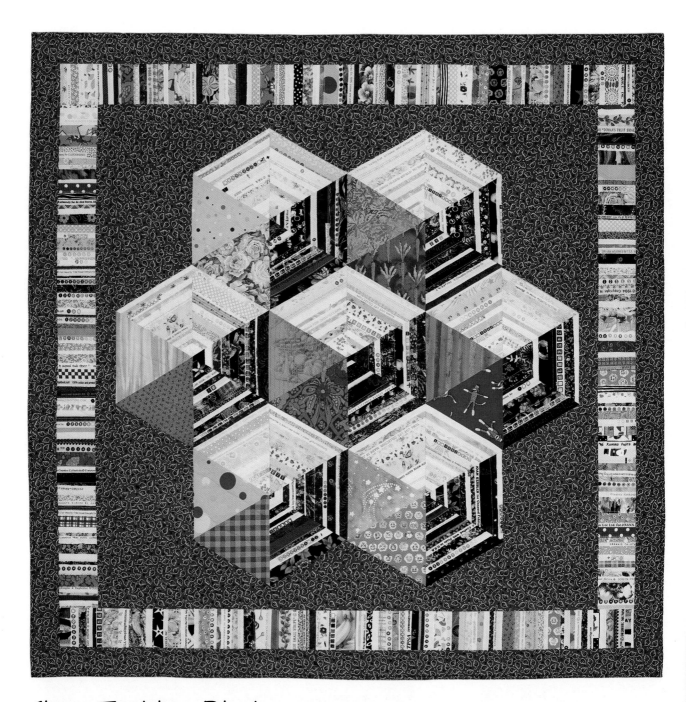

# Glass Tumbling Blocks • 48" x 49" • *Made and quilted by the author*

I love the optical illusion of a Tumbling Blocks design. I think the use of selvages enhances this effect because the stripes delineate the edges of the blocks. You can see into the blocks as if you are looking down from above. You can also look into the blocks from the right or from the left. The use of darks, lights, and mediums is particularly important in this quilt. I was glad to have some very dark selvages to use, especially some that have no white stripe at all. In the medium areas, I chose some batik fabrics to create a translucent glow. If you repeat your background fabric on your outer border, the selvage border will appear to float. I also used the background fabric for the binding.

## Foundation Fabric for Selvage-covered Triangles and Border

1½ yards

*Cut into:* **(4) 6¾" x 40" strips,** then cut 28 equilateral triangles.

**(5) 3½" x 40" strips**

## Tumbling Block Triangle

Medium Batiks — ½ yard

*Cut into:* **(2) 6¾" x 40" strips,** cut 14 equilateral triangles.

## Background, Inner & Outer Border

Medium value — 1¼ yards

*Cut into:* Background **(3) 6¾" x 40" strips,** then cut 24 equilateral triangles.

Inner Border: **(4) 2" x 40" strips**

Outer Border: **(5) 2½" x 40" strips**

## Straight-grain Double-fold Binding

Medium Value — ½ yard

*Cut into:* **(5) 2½" x 40" strips**

## Quilt Backing

3½ yards

*Cut into:* **(2) 1¾ yard lengths**

## Batting

56" x 57"

### *Sewing Instructions*

Cover 14 foundation fabric triangles using very light selvages, as shown in Making Equilateral Triangles (page 22). Remember to lay the selvages parallel to the straight-of-grain edge of the triangles.

Cover 14 foundation fabric triangles using your darkest selvages.

Cut 14 triangles from fabrics of medium value.
This is easier to do than trying to make selvage combinations of a medium value. You may want to fussy-cut triangles from different fabrics.

Arrange your pieces on a design wall according to the layout diagram or until you have an effect that pleases you. Fill in the medium-value background triangles.

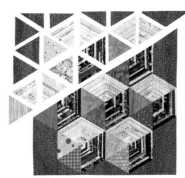

Imagine each individual Tumbling Block as a pie. Notice how each slice is pointing toward the center with the light, medium, and dark triangles adjacent to each other and in the same position relative to all the other "pies."

The Tumbling Blocks will stand out best if you choose a background fabric that is darker than your light selvages, but lighter than your dark selvages. That is to say, audition your whole stash until one fabric says, "Yes!"

Sew the triangles into diagonal rows, then join the rows. Trim the zigzag edges to make your quilt top square, and add an inner border of 2" background fabric strips.

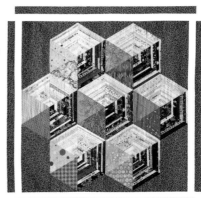

Cover the 3½" wide foundation fabric strips as shown in Making Long Blocks (page 21) with selvages of all colors and values.

Piece as necessary and add to the sides and top and bottom of the quilt, and add the outer border of 2½" background strips.

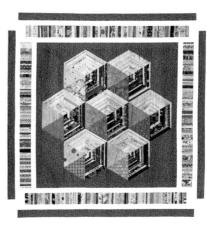

Layer the quilt top with the backing and batting and quilt. Square up the quilt top and use the 2½" strips to bind the raw edges of your quilt.

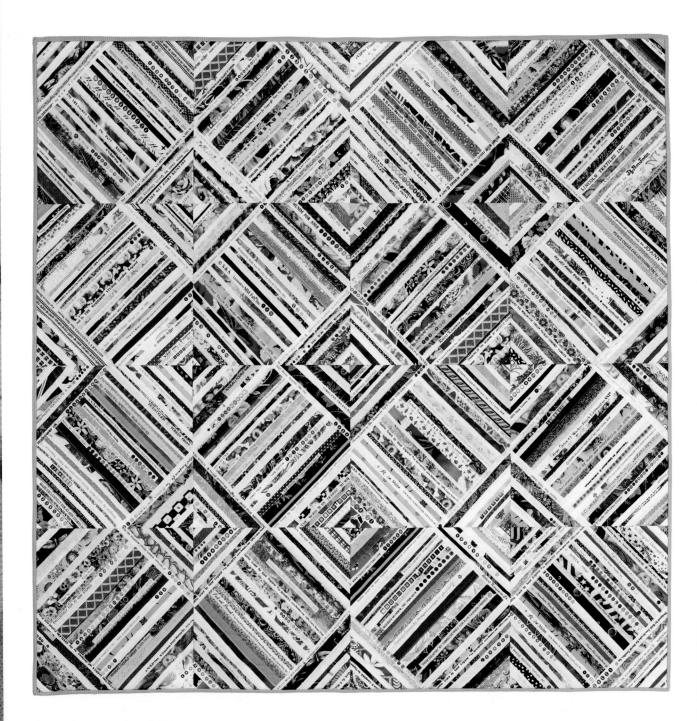

# Acres of Afternoon • 49" x 49" • *Made and quilted by the author*

This quilt is very busy, but curiously satisfying. The eye can wander around for a long time in this playful quilt, like a child enjoying a long afternoon outdoors.

The lime green binding and bits of lime green among the selvages work together to create a cheerful sparkle.

**Foundation Blocks**

2¼ yards

*Cut into:* (16) 12½" squares

**Straight-grain Double-fold Binding**

Lime Green — ½ yard

*Cut into:* (5) 2½" x 40" strips

**Quilt Back**

3½ yards

*Cut into:* (2) 1¾ yard lengths

**Batting**

57" x 57"

## Sewing Instructions

Draw guidelines on the muslin squares by first drawing both diagonals. Then draw two lines parallel to one diagonal halfway between the diagonal line and the corners of the square, as shown.

Sew selvages onto the foundation diagonally.

Add selvages to the two empty corners.

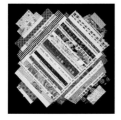

Precision is not necessary here. You might want to put these blocks on the design wall as you make them, so that you can see what direction you want the words to read. Some of your selvages will read upside-down.

Trim the finished block to 12" square. Make 16.

Arrange in 4 rows of 4 blocks each, alternating the orientation of the blocks as shown. Sew the blocks into rows, then join the rows.

Use a walking foot to help handle the bulk.

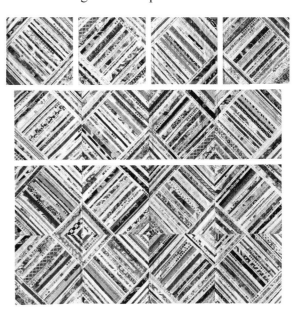

Layer the quilt top with the backing and batting and quilt. Square up the quilt top and use the 2½" strips to bind the raw edges of your quilt.

## Log Cabin, Heart's Desire • 51" x 51" • *Made and quilted by the author*

No collection of quilts is complete without a Log Cabin quilt, a Barn Raising version in particular. I think the classic red hearths look especially nice in this quilt because they are framed by white selvages on all four sides. A satisfying Log Cabin quilt has always thrilled my heart.

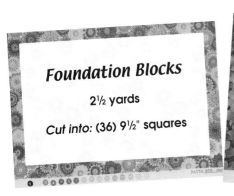

**Foundation Blocks**

2½ yards

*Cut into:* (36) 9½" squares

**Block Centers & Straight-grain Double-fold Binding**

Red — ⅞ yard

*Cut into:* (36) 2½" x 2½" squares

(6) 2½" x 40" strips

© LAKEHOUSE LH 03011 "Hydrangea Blossom" WWW.LAKEHOUSEDIRECT.COM

**Quilt Back**

3½ yards

*Cut into:* (2) 1¾ yard lengths

**Batting**

59" x 59"

### Sewing Instructions

Lay a red 2½" square in the center of a 9½" muslin square. Do this "by eye."

Lay a selvage on top of one edge of the red square, as in the illustration below.

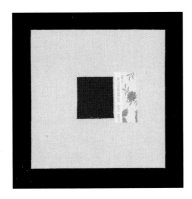

Start with a dark selvage on some blocks and start with a light selvage on other blocks. This gives a less precise, more interesting, improvisational look to your quilt.

Add selvages, working two adjacent sides of the block in lights, and the other two sides in darks, as shown. Press as necessary.

Don't worry if you get an uneven number of dark and light rows, as in the quilt photo. Again, I think this adds interest.

Trim the finished blocks to 9" square.

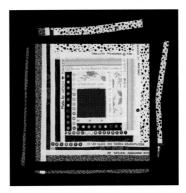

Arrange in 6 rows of 6 blocks each in a Barn Raising pattern by turning the dark and light corners to form the large diamond shapes.

Sew into rows, and then sew the rows together.

Layer the quilt top with the backing and batting and quilt. Square up the quilt top and use the 2½" strips to bind the raw edges of your quilt.

QUILTS FROM THE SELVAGE EDGE

Karen Griska

# Remembering Silk Cigar Ribbon Quilts • 39" x 39" • *Made and quilted by the author*

In the late 1800s and early 1900s, cigars were sold in bundles, wrapped in silk ribbons that were marked with the cigar manufacturer's name. There were thousands of brands to choose from, so competition was lively and the ribbons were beautifully designed. It was popular to collect these ribbons and use them for pillow covers, table covers, and quilts.

Many times, I have thought that using selvages in a quilt is a lot like using silk cigar ribbons. Of course,

unlike silk ribbons, only one edge of a selvage strip is a bound edge, so we need to cover up the raw edge. However, the writing on a selvage is more interesting to us than the names of cigar companies!

In this quilt I have attempted to arrange my selvages in a way that is reminiscent of these antiques. I think the embroidery, beading, and crocheted edge add to the antique charm of this quilt.

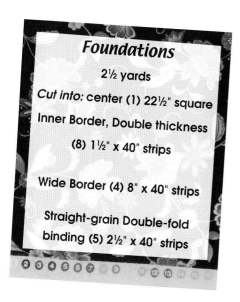

**Foundations**

2½ yards

*Cut into:* center (1) 22½" square

Inner Border, Double thickness

(8) 1½" x 40" strips

Wide Border (4) 8" x 40" strips

Straight-grain Double-fold
binding (5) 2½" x 40" strips

*Note: The muslin inner border strips and binding are not covered by selvages. Only 1¾ yards of "uglies" can be substituted for the muslin.*

**Quilt Back**

2¾ yards

*Cut into:* (2) 1⅜ yard lengths

**Batting**

47" x 47"

BASIX – C6236

## Directions

Draw guidelines on the 22" square of foundation fabric as shown. Cover the center square with selvages, one at a time, sewing down after each addition.

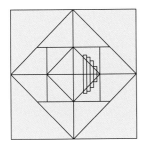

Cover the raw ends of the center section by covering two opposite corner triangles with selvages, then the other two corners.

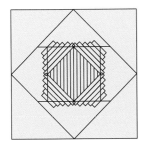

Cover the raw ends of these sections by adding selvages to the next sections as shown.

Add selvages to the corners. Trim the finished center block to 22" square. Add a border using a double layer of the 1½" muslin strips so the thickness of the border will be compatible with the rest of the quilt.

From the 8" wide strips, cut two strips 25". Cover these two strips and the two 40" strips with selvages as shown in Making Long Blocks (page 21).

Measure the length of the quilt through the center, and cut the 25" covered strips to that measurement. Add to the sides of the quilt.

Measure the width of the quilt through the center, and cut the 40" covered strips to that measurement. Add to the top and bottom of the quilt. Add embroidery and beads to the double-muslin inner border. Layer the quilt top with the backing and batting and quilt. Square up the quilt top and use the 2½" strips to bind the raw edges. A crocheted edge was added to the binding.

QUILTS FROM THE SELVAGE EDGE

Karen Griska

# Tulip's Apron

*These instructions are for the apron I made for Mark Lipinski's dog, Tulip. The instructions are for a dog of 13-16 pounds but can easily be adapted for a larger dog.*

### Apron Ties

Ribbon — 2 yards

Cut into: (4) ½ yard pieces

### Apron Foundation

Felt Squares

Cut: (2) 8" x 10" squares

### Apron Front

White letter beads

Spell the dog's name.

## Directions

Enlarge and trace the apron pattern.

Butt the two squares of felt and zig-zag stitch them together.

Trace the apron pattern onto the felt and cut it out.

Starting at the bottom of the apron, lay the first selvage at the edge and topstitch the bound edge to the apron. Let all the selvage ends hang off the foundation about 1" on each side.

Lay the next selvage so that its bound edge overlaps the raw edge of the first. Sew along the bound edge of the second selvage. Continue adding selvage strips to the top of the apron, letting the raw edge of the last one to hang over the top.

Turn the apron over and trim the selvages to about ½" all the way around. Fold the selvage ends over onto the back of the apron. Clip to ease the foldovers in the curved "armhole" areas.

Press. Topstitch around the outer edge of the apron about ¼" from the edge.

Attach two pieces of ribbon to the top of the apron bib and two at the "waist."

Hand sew the little beads to personalize the apron for the canine recipient.

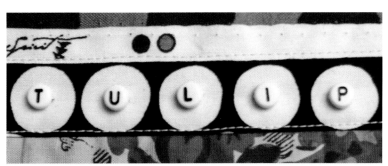

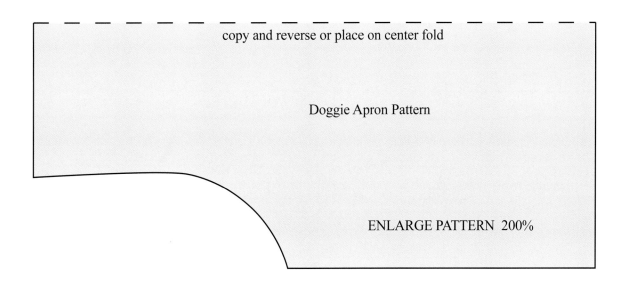

copy and reverse or place on center fold

Doggie Apron Pattern

ENLARGE PATTERN 200%

# What About Finishing?

## How do you apply borders?

Square up the quilt top. Measure the length of the quilt through the center. Cut two border strips to that measurement and add to the sides of the quilt. Press the seam allowance toward the border.

Measure the width of the quilt through the center, including the side borders. Cut two border strips to that measurement and add to the top and bottom of the quilt. Press the seam allowance toward the border.

## Are selvage quilt tops too thick for batting and quilting?

No. All of the quilts in this book have low-loft cotton batting and are machine quilted. They feel very nice and are not particularly thick.

## What is the best way to quilt a selvage top?

I do straight line machine quilting using a walking foot. This is a special foot that moves the top layer of the quilt at the same speed as the backing so the sandwich doesn't shift. I quilt wavy parallel lines. That way, I can avoid quilting over any bulky seam intersections. Square up the quilt when the quilting is complete.

## What about binding?

Each pattern calls for straight-of-grain 2½" binding strips. Join them end-to-end with a diagonal seam. Press the seam allowances open, then fold in half lengthwise, right sides together, and press. Matching the raw edges with the edge of the quilt, sew around the quilt with a ¼" seam. Turn to the back and hand finish.

## Does my quilt need a hanging sleeve?

Even if you plan to use your quilt on a bed or as a throw, you may want to hang it in the future. It is easier and neater to add the sleeve before the binding goes on. The fabric requirements given for backing include enough for a sleeve.

## What about a label?

You don't want your quilt to end up in a museum someday with "Maker Unknown" given all the credit.

## Should I photograph my quilt?

Yes! Visit www.SelvageQuilts.com and click on Gallery, then Exhibit to send me a picture of your selvage quilt.

# Resources

Smith, Loretta. *Pineapple Quilt, A Piece of Cake*. San Marcos, California: Quilt in a Day, 1989.

Visit www.cranstonvillage.com for an online tour of the fabric manufacturing process. Click on About Us and select How Our Fabric Is Made.

# About the Author

Karen Griska is a passionate and prolific quilt artist who made her first quilt at age 13, a charming one-patch. A self-taught quilter, she has now made over 200 quilts, all original designs. Karen is inspired by antique quilts, particularly those pictured in the state quilt survey books, which she studies avidly. Her favorites are dynamic interpretations of traditional quilts. She loves quilts with quirky, improvisational elements of surprise in their design.

Her favorite part of the quiltmaking process is creating the design. Karen does not usually sketch a plan in advance, but prefers to develop the design as she works. The thrill of discovery fuels her passion for quilting. She would rather quilt than eat!

Karen enjoys encouraging other quilters to have more fun with their quilting. She challenges them to ignore precision in piecing and coordinating fabrics in favor of working in a more carefree style. She created the Oregon Trail Quilt Challenge, in which quilters make a small quilt using only a given bundle of fabrics and no pattern. "What," she asks, "would you make if you were out on the Oregon Trail and could use only the materials you had on hand and the ideas in your head?"

Karen gives lectures and workshops on Creativity in Quilting, Improvisational Sampler Quilts, and Dynamic String Quilts and teaches a variety of inventive classes utilizing selvages. You can read more about Karen at www. RealWomenQuilt.com in the Featured Quilter-Archives section. For more on selvage quilts, go to Karen's new Web site, www.selvagequilts.com. She is eager to see your selvage quilts and invites you to exhibit photos of your own selvage art in her gallery.

Karen and her husband currently reside in White Plains, New York.

# Other AQS Books

This is only a small selection of the books available from the American Quilter's Society. AQS books are known worldwide for timely topics, clear writing, beautiful color photos, and accurate illustrations and patterns. The following books are available from your local bookseller, quilt shop, or public library.

#7601     US$26.95

#4995     US$19.95

#7490     US$22.95

#7605     US$24.95

#7615     US$24.95

#7611     US$26.95

#7487     US$19.95

#7491     US$22.95

#7484     US$22.95

**Look** for these books nationally.
**Call** or **Visit** our Web site at

# 1-800-626-5420
**www.AmericanQuilter.com**